Poetic Voices

Poetic Voices

POETIC VOICES

Seeking Solidarity During Racial Transitions

A Collaboration With:
Angela R. Edwards
&
Marlowe R. Scott

Pearly Gates Publishing, LLC, Houston, Texas (USA)

Poetic Voices

Poetic Voices:
Seeking Solidarity During Racial Transitions

Copyright © 2020
Angela R. Edwards and Marlowe R. Scott

All Rights Reserved.
No portion of this publication may be reproduced, stored in an electronic system, or transmitted in any form or by any means (electronic, mechanical, photocopy, recording, or otherwise) without written permission from the authors or publisher. Brief quotations may be used in literary reviews.

Print ISBN 13: 978-1-948853-04-0
Digital ISBN 13: 978-1-948853-05-7
Library of Congress Control Number: 2020944789

Scripture is taken from the King James Version (KJV) of the Holy Bible and used with permission via Zondervan at Biblegateway.com. Public Domain.

For information and bulk ordering, contact:
Pearly Gates Publishing, LLC
Angela Edwards, CEO
P.O. Box 62287
Houston, TX 77205
BestSeller@PearlyGatesPublishing.com

Poetic Voices

Dedication

Too many names to share in this book.
Too many names…have you looked?
The pain is felt across the globe.
When it will stop?
Only God knows.

Poetic Voices
is dedicated to the countless memories
of lives lost during some of the most turbulent
times in our **world's** history.

"The World"
might have failed us, but **GOD** never will.

A portion of proceeds from the sales of this book will benefit Color of Change.

Poetic Voices

Acknowledgments

First, giving all glory, honor, and praise to our Heavenly Father. It was He who gave the vision and mission to compile this piece of literary art. As obedient servants, those who are here answered His call.

To my Mother, **Marlowe R. Scott:** Thank you for always being 100% authentically *YOU*. You have raised your children in the ways of the Lord and set in each of us the mindset that **NO ONE** is better than us, no matter how highly they may think of themselves—and, in turn, we are no better than another. I, for one, appreciate your gentle and constant reminders that the Bible says we are **ALL** God's children—not just the select few who may think otherwise. I love you to the moon and beyond!

To each of the Contributors to this amazing project: You showed up and showed out! From the youngest to the oldest, each of you have given a voice to some of your innermost secrets, all for the purpose of affecting change…*NOW*. Thank you for your willingness to bear your heart and soul on the pages of this book. You are **ALL** to be commended!

To the two special women in my life who penned the Forewords for *Poetic Voices*, **Laurie Benoit** and **Sabrina Williams:** Thank you for answering the call to sow your hearts into this project without the least bit of hesitation. The viewpoints each of you share are as unique as you are and speak valuable truths the **WORLD** needs to know. Blessings to you both, today and always!

Poetic Voices

Poetic Contributions By:
(in order of appearance)

Brandon Jamal White *(Artist)*

Aniyah K. Williams

Jai'saiah M. Green

Kelyce L. Williams

Tayler Wright-Williams

Gerald Savage, III

Arlene Holden

Tosha Dearbone

Carl Reid

Angela R. Edwards

Terrace White

Marlowe R. Scott

John Hansboro

Terrance Bernard

Keywana Wright

Poetless Shakespeare

Marilyn E. Porter

Poetic Voices

Foreword by International (Canadian) Advocate

~ Author Laurie Benoit @ Once Awakened ~

****

Dedication

To all my brothers and sisters of humankind:

May **KINDNESS** follow you on every path you travel.
May **PEACE** be present in your heart and soul every day.
May **PATIENCE** be found in challenging moments.
May **GENTLENESS** be conveyed in both actions and words.
May **UNDERSTANDING** be ever-present in each passing moment.
May **LOVE** find you in every corner of the world.

****

Bio

Laurie Benoit is a wife, mother of four, and a grandmother. She is author of the International Best-Selling book, *The Transformative Power of "The Word,"* and has made contributions to other literary works, including: *God Says I am Battle-Scar Free: Testimonies of Abuse Survivors (Parts 4, 5, and 6), God's Joy Fruit: Walking Through the Fields of Grace and Mercy in Bloom,* and *God's Love Fruit: Walking Through the Fields of Grace and Mercy in Bloom.* Laurie is an avid photographer, mentor, Contributing Writer for "Scars of Survival" Magazine, and an ever-learning student of life.

Poetic Voices

The first thing I wish to express is how deeply humbled and truly honored I feel, having been asked to write this Foreword.

Thank you, my beautiful sister from my other mother, for this amazing opportunity to be part of the change I wish to see.

Namaste!

No, my sister and I are not related. No, we are not from the same country. No, we are not even the same color.

We are sisters who believe in the power of the word.

We are sisters who believe change is possible.

We are sisters who believe in fair treatment and justice.

We are sisters who believe in kindness and love for all.

ABOVE ALL ELSE, we are sisters for humanity...*ALL* humanity alike—no matter your age, caste, height, weight, appearance, disability, family status, gender identity or expression, marital status, nationality, ethnicity, religion, sex, political ideology, or social class.

Often, as we grow through life, we will come across at least one person who will use one thing to discriminate against us from one of the topics above. Why is that? Quite frankly, it is something I have simply just never been able to fathom. See, to me, there may be little or even a great many differences in

Poetic Voices

each one of us but overall, I believe we are all very much the same.

HOWEVER, if anyone truly understood the full depth of my story, they might begin to understand why, in this day and age, I appreciate *ALL* people — even the ones we must learn hard lessons from.

Ever since I was a young child, I have always known I was different. "The black sheep of the family" is what I was called. Why? Because I was never one to just be okay with the less-than-mediocre treatment I endured. As a young child, I knew the things that happened to me were wrong. As a result, I quickly learned there was only one person who would come to my defense. Me.

So, how did I learn so quickly, you might wonder? Well, the very people who should have protected me were the very reason for my terrors. Then, after finding my way into a system I thought would have my best interests at heart, what I didn't know was that I had many more valuable lessons ahead of me. See, when I was a young girl, I learned my words had power — which was why I was abruptly silenced. Every which way I turned, my words were dismissed as quickly as I spoke them.

Here's the thing: When you speak up and out against injustice, people do **NOT** want to hear the truth. It has been my experience that a normal reaction is, *"If we ignore it, it will just go away…"*

It doesn't, though.

Poetic Voices

Instead, that truth goes on, unheard in someone's heart and mind for what might seem like or, in fact, be a lifetime…until they have an opportunity to talk about it and 'IT' is truly validated. Isn't that it? Don't we need to feel heard? We do, after all, need some sort of validation that lets us know we are not crazy, that someone really hears us, and that what we feel and went through is authentic.

Our words matter. They matter to us and to others who have been through what we, too, have endured…or are enduring.

One other thing I have also learned along the way is that every single word you utter can **NEVER** be unsaid.

When we truly look at things with openness, we will observe it's not the words spoken that destroy people. Rather, it's *people* who destroy people.

Honestly, it breaks my heart that, more often than not, we humans care more about what we can gain from hurting and railroading others, than what we gain by giving of ourselves to help each other.

Another truth of mine is "Life Isn't Fair," especially for those who have spoken out against injustice. Please think about this: Is that really what life is supposed to be about? I hope not! What would be the point of fighting for a cause, then?

Admittedly, life does not need to continue on the same course of action. It is only through determination, courage, awareness, and a willingness to strive towards becoming a

Poetic Voices

better person, that each one of us can begin to make the world a better place. We live in an era when there is a great deal more worldwide awareness about the significant number of issues that affect people daily. How is it that humanity has not overcome any of them? Will we ever? I would like to think so. Even more, I would truly like to believe it.

Somewhere in the back of my mind lies a harrowing version of that truth...

It is my belief that politicians and the media worldwide instigate and magnify a great many number of issues to the benefit of those who should not necessarily be protected. Meanwhile, those in dire need of care and support are being turned away or fall through the cracks. In my opinion, it is because of both the governments of the world and media that it usually takes public outcry or a large number of people fighting for a cause to make change possible.

When are we going to learn we are all brothers and sisters of humanity? It is only when we truly begin to show and act with love and care towards our brothers and sisters that we will see change. Only through **SOLIDARITY** of humankind will we find the answers to our questions.

Can one person really make that much of a difference?

As I ask myself that question today, the universe provided me with an answer: **YES!** One person **CAN** make a difference! So, please: I invite you...I *implore* you to make your difference today!

Poetic Voices

Foreword by Baltimore, Maryland (USA) Advocate

~ Sabrina Williams @ Sistas N Strength Support Group ~

SOLIDARITY. RACIAL. TRANSITION. Three words that represent strength, courage, and commitment.

The meaning of **SOLIDARITY** is "unity or agreement of feeling or action, especially among people with a common interest."

The meaning of **RACIAL** is "relating to a race."

The meaning of **TRANSITION** is "the process of changing from one state or condition to another."

This book contains all three meanings. Through poetry, each writer's experiences and feelings are solidified in words.

It is truly my honor to contribute to this book by writing this Foreword, as this is my first experience doing so. I was excited when my friend, Angela Edwards, asked me to pen these words. I was also nervous.

As I meditated on the title, memories from the past flooded my thoughts—particularly of the torture endured by our ancestors during the Transatlantic Slave Trade, the oppression of the Jim Crow Laws, the Civil Rights Movement, and even the injustices of the Black race still endured today.

Poetic Voices

Yet through it all, we remain strong and courageous as we continue to fight for a better way of life.

I found myself inhaling and exhaling as I focused on how I met my friend, Angela. Our introduction was a bit of solidarity. We "met" on Twitter. I would promote my client's business, and she would retweet my tweets. I did not know who she was, but appreciated her efforts, nonetheless. In the busy environment of Twitter, her retweets encouraged me to keep pushing for my client. Soon after, she and I connected and built a friendship.

At the time, Angela had her first business: Angela's Accurate Administrative Services. As our friendship grew, I learned she was the CEO and Chief Editorial Director of her publishing company, Pearly Gates Publishing, LLC. Our friendship continued to develop, and we supported each other. It did not matter that we lived many miles away from one another—she in Texas, and I in Maryland. Regardless of the distance, she and I developed a bond that bridged us in solidarity and strengthened our love and support for each other through life's transitions. It was Angela's passion for helping writers and publishing books that inspired me to venture into a new project to help independent authors.

Our support for each other grew strong in a relatively short amount of time. I would support her publishing endeavor by referring people who needed a publisher or expressed interest in writing a book. I also donated to her community-based endeavors. In turn, she would support me by donating to my annual Socks Drive and School Uniform Drive, as well as supporting my entertainment endeavors. We even partnered in

Poetic Voices

community outreach projects to help residents in our respective cities.

From my friendship with Angela, I met her mother, Mrs. Marlowe Scott. Mom Marlowe (as I call her) is an author of several books. She is a loving, caring, and support person. By getting to know Mom Marlowe, I learned why Angela and I instantly connected. Both are loving, caring, strong, supportive, and harmonious women, which is why their collaboration to produce a book on this topic comes as no surprise to me.

Poetry... I have always had a love for the art. I can't recall precisely when it first caught my attention, though. It may have been after reading poems by Phyllis Wheatley, Maya Angelou, or Langston Hughes. There is this one thing that rings true: Poems touched my soul and stirred my spirit.

As a youth, I was in love with Hip-Hop music, and reading poems was like sweet icing on my Hip-Hop cake. That is one reason I'm honored to write this Foreword. Poetry and Hip-Hop are brethren...kindred souls, if you will. Poetry is rich with one's experiences, feelings, and truth. Just like music, it is universal! It seeps into the souls of people, touching their hearts with each line. It destroys boundaries and transitions differences into similarities.

Words have many powers. They hold a strong, important power—a vital force in our lives.

Words have the **power** to heal.

Words have the **power** to unify.

Poetic Voices

Words have the **power** to teach and bring understanding.

Words have the **power** to soothe the spirit.

Words have the **power** to give strength.

Most importantly, words have the **power** to make change!

As you read this book, I pray the words of each writer give you that *POWER*! I pray you receive what is needed to ignite a fiery, white-hot flame of solidarity with others, just like it ignited one among Angela, Mom Marlowe, and me.

In closing, I share with you the slogan of a community-based group I founded:

"Together, We Can Make a Change and Be the Change!"

Stay lifted!

Poetic Voices

Introduction

So many voices are being heard today, but what are they saying? They are speaking about racism, inequality, and Black Lives Matter. Most recently, perhaps the newest voices cry out, "All Lives Matter."

The National Black Anthem, "Lift Every Voice and Sing," composed by James Weldon Johnson and J. Rosamond Johnson, seems more appropriate now than ever.

> "Lift ev'ry voice and sing,
> 'Til earth and heaven ring;
> Ring with the harmonies of Liberty.
> Let our rejoicing rise,
> High as the list'ning skies.
> Let it resound loud as the rolling sea.
> Sing a song full of the faith that the dark past has taught us.
> Sing a song full of the hope that the present has brought us.
> Facing the rising sun of our new day begun.
> Let us march on 'til victory is won!"
>
> Source: www.naacp.org/naacp-history-lift-evry-voice-and-sing/

Various American ethnicities and even those from far away countries have joined the voices with rallies and demonstrations. There has arisen a need for overdue change in their lives, laws, police force actions, years of historical unfairness in crime punishments, and so much more.

Poetic Voices

What is the cause of the raised voices, one might ask? It is the murder of one Black man in the United States who was choked by an armed policeman while two of his fellow officers not only watched, but also held the choking man on the ground!

Since that dreadful day, small changes in laws and human rights have been adopted and passed.

This battle, however, is far from over.

Enter in *Poetic Voices*. Poetry is a perfect means of expressing one's feelings and shared experiences, whether they be past, present, or an anticipated future. The poetry compositions in this collaboration cover a wide variety of raw adult memories and those of childhood experiences. Others will share rays of hope, while others will utter hopelessness.

A very exciting and inspiring portion of *Poetic Voices* highlights four of today's young voices! Even at their young age, they, too, have experienced incidents simply because of the color of their skin. Their words surely will touch your soul! As you read them, whenever it is possible, use them to encourage the youth you meet to share those times when they are or have been discriminated against. Help them seek the equality each of us deserve!

There are five very distinct goals of *Poetic Voices*. They are as diverse as the composers of each literary piece.

1. To bring **AWARENESS** of abuses and inequalities toward minority people throughout recorded history.

Poetic Voices

2. To shed enlightened **AWARENESS** of incidents leading to today's marches, riots, and peaceful demonstrations.
3. To bring **AWARENESS** to the fact that some who are meant to protect members of society do not always perform their duties in fairness to different ethnic groups—primarily Blacks.
4. To bring **AWARENESS** to those who still support the historical and continual abuses inflicted on minorities.
5. *IMPORTANT:* To **ACKNOWLEDGE** the one man who, though now dead, made a difference in our lives by his *murder*!

As you read, there may be a tear shed. You may even find yourself embracing feelings of anger. Be aware that acting in haste or hatred is not the best reaction. Instead, you are encouraged to join an organization that is actively involved in change and equality for our fellow man…and woman. Volunteer your time, talents, and funds (if available) to further the cause to which you are dedicated.

Read literature about Black History (there are countless books available in libraries and online).

Educate *YOURSELF*. Don't rely on just what you are and have been told through the media. There are lies being told daily, as well as ethnic abuses and inhumane practices, throughout the world.

Finally, as you have the opportunity, share what you discover on the pages of this book with others—especially our youth. They need to know what has happened, is happening,

Poetic Voices

and what is ahead as they prepare to carry the torch for
LIBERTY AND JUSTICE FOR ALL!

Poetic Voices

Table of Contents

Dedication vi
Acknowledgments vii
Poetic Contributions By: viii
Foreword by International (Canadian) Advocate ix
Foreword by Baltimore, Maryland (USA) Advocate xiv
Introduction xviii
The Youth Speak 1
The Use-*HER* 2
   Aniyah K. Williams
The Black Kid 4
   Jai'saiah M. Green
I Thought She Was My Friend 7
   Kelyce L. Williams
I am A Black Girl! 9
   Tayler Wright-Williams
Adult Voices: Shouldering the Task 11
Solidarity 12
   Gerald Savage, III
If You Only Knew Who I Am 14
   Arlene Holden
Black Woman Systematically 17
   Tosha Dearbone
My Racially Mixed-Up Journey 19
   Carl Reid
Melting Pot 20
   Angela R. Edwards

Poetic Voices

A Prayer for a Brighter Day 21
   Terrace White

The Tenacity To… 23
   Angela R. Edwards

HANDS UP! 25
   Marlowe R. Scott

#45 27
   John Hansboro

The DIAMOND of DIAMONDS 30
   Terrance Bernard

A Mother's Prayer 32
   Keywana Wright

Battle Tone 34
   Poetless Shakespeare

Dying Words 36
   Marlowe R. Scott

Fast-Forward to 2021 37
   Marilyn E. Porter

Who Would Have Dreamed It? 38
   Marlowe R. Scott

Conclusion 40

Meet the Collaborators 42
   Angela R. Edwards 42
   Marlowe R. Scott 46

Pen A Poem 50

Poetic Voices

Original Artwork by Brandon Jamal White © June 2020

Poetic Voices

The Youth Speak

Poetic Voices

The Use-*HER*
Aniyah K. Williams

Aniyah Williams is a bright and talented nine-year-old who loves to write, dance, and make friends. She is the second oldest of four girls and has two furbaby dogs that she adores. In her free time, she showers her baby sister with love, helps her mom around the house, and travels with her family. Aniyah is the granddaughter of Angela Edwards and great-granddaughter of Marlowe Scott.

Poetic Voices

Friends for years…

Or so I thought.

She used me for what I had to give;

I knew it, but chose to forgive.

Time went on and I was replaced

By someone who I thought I could trust.

The lesson I learned early on

Is that self-love is a **MUST**.

She turned her back on me

And wouldn't even speak.

After all, she must have thought that

Because I am Black, I was the one beneath.

I was used by "The Use-HER,"

But now, I realize it was better to **LOSE-HER.**

Poetic Voices

The Black Kid
Jai'saiah M. Green

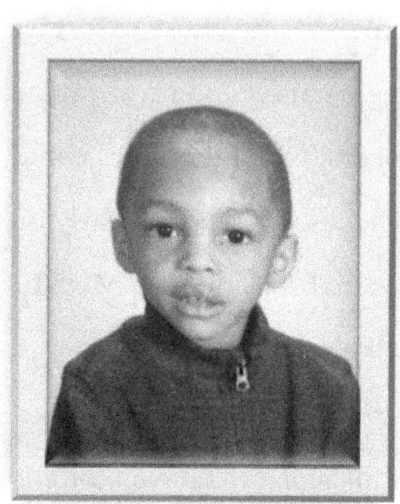

Jai'saiah M. Green is a seven-year-old African American male who loves learning, school, games, and spending time with his mother and grandmother. Presently, he is in the second grade. During these times, being a Black kid in America is not normal because of all the racial stereotypes in society that are unjust and unknown, leaving him to desire remaining a kid and learning about his life as one. He appreciates the teachings of T.D. Jakes because he shares the Word of God in a way in which he can relate and believes God will one day cure racial injustice.

READ ISAIAH 66:13 & PROVERBS 31:26

Jai'saiah dedicates his poem to every child who must endure social injustices due to racism or mistreatment just because they are "The Black Kid."

Poetic Voices

To be a Black Kid in America has a blank, scarred mark without God. The treasure of the land is being honest and smart. Well, let me speak straight from the heart.

Black is a color, but it is what I am with the skin tone,
But God didn't create racism for us to condone.
There are points to this pose,
Being The Black Kid during racial injustices, while Whites turn up their nose.

Can you ask God to protect His children from the violence of social injustice? We are diverse because of His blood.

I am The Black Kid.

Racial injustices for kids are harmful to us,
Yet all we can do is pray, fast, and let God lead us.
I am my brother's keeper during these times
Of being The Black Kid to have in mind.

Continue to be mighty and fight, kids!
We shall overcome this season of change some day.

The changes of the world being a Black Kid came long ago with Rev. Dr. Martin Luther King and the movements of freedom leaders that showed up to give.

God loves us all; big, Black, little, or small.
Why should being Black matter at all?
When God created the world, He had no choice of color for any of us. He shaped, molded, and created us in His image so that nothing could change the world but Him.

Poetic Voices

Being The Black Kid sometimes in the eyes of the world
Means no good to others but is ordained by the Word.
Stand in unity so we can change the world!
Being The Black Kid is not so bad.

Growing up being Black, my mother has kept me safe from all that "stuff" that kept a target on my back —
The knowledge and education of what police brutality looked like for children or Blacks who had White knees on their necks.

Kids are not aware of the systems of others being cruel because we are just kids.
In our society, how can we get clarity to live our liberty for justice to have a chance at unity?

I am The Black Kid.

Poetic Voices

I Thought She Was My Friend
Kelyce L. Williams

Kelyce Williams is a bright-eyed seven-year-old and third oldest of four sisters. She has a kind heart and a gentle, "old" soul. When she's not hard at work teaching her baby sister new things, she enjoys eating, making TikTok videos, and playing around with her two furbaby dogs. Kelyce is the granddaughter of Angela Edwards and great-granddaughter of Marlowe Scott.

Poetic Voices

We would be in school,

And she treated me like a fool.

All the time, she smiled in my face.

When I turned my back, it was a disgrace.

Her White skin and Brown hair

Made her think she was better than me.

She even told my other friends,

"Prejudiced is the way to be!"

I thought she was my friend,

But I guess I was wrong.

Still, I love **MY** Black skin

And will always be strong.

Poetic Voices

I am A Black Girl!
Tayler Wright-Williams

Tayler Wright-Williams is 10 years old and an author of her own book, *I Like My Lip Balm*. She resides in Flint, Michigan, with her mother, Keywana Wright. She is a "B" Honor Roll student who most recently passed to the 4th Grade. Tayler enjoys school and playing with her friends, basketball, video games, and watching Disney shows. Her favorite foods are fried chicken and pizza.

Poetic Voices

I am a Black Girl who is proud of my brown skin.

I am a Black Girl who is smart and courageous.

I am a Black Girl who enjoys laughing and telling jokes.

I am a Black Girl who cries aloud when I am hurt.

I am a Black Girl who thinks I am a Supergirl with powers to help another girl who is powerless.

I am a Black Girl who believes in myself.

I can be whatever I want to be.

I am a Black Girl who is proud of who I am.

Poetic Voices

Adult Voices: Shouldering the Task

Poetic Voices

Solidarity
Gerald Savage, III

Gerald Savage, III is a New Jersey native and father of one son named Porter. Presently, he serves in the United States Army as a Staff Sergeant, with plans to go career. He holds a degree in General Studies from University of Maryland University College and is pursuing a Bachelor's in Cybersecurity. Gerald is the only son of Angela Edwards and one of two grandsons of Marlowe R. Scott.

Poetic Voices

Unity or agreement of feeling or action.
Why is this idea just gaining traction?
A man had to die over a $20.00 transaction;
Now, Black Lives Matter is the latest fashion.

We just all want to live in prosperity,
But why is there so much disparity?
Can you please provide some clarity?
Why is compassion such a rarity?

Together, we can win this fight
So that every man and woman can have the right
To walk comfortably in the daylight…
Without the greatest fear being police lights.

Poetic Voices

If You Only Knew Who I Am
Arlene Holden

I was born a Black child.
I looked like any other baby,
Only my skin was brown.
Did that make a difference? Maybe.

I started school when I was five,
I missed my mom…and I cried and cried.
Why don't we all look alike?
God made us that way, and He does things right.

God created us for His glory.
If you read your Bible, it will tell the story.
God made us from one blood;
It remained the same, even after the flood.

When I went to school,
I often heard the "N" word.
In our house,
That word was seldom heard.
Nice people didn't talk like that,
I was taught.

If You Only Knew Who I Am.

I had some classmates
Who were White.
We got along;
We didn't fight.

Poetic Voices

I had a teacher who enjoyed reading
"Old Black Joe" and "Black Sambo."
Did those stories enhance our intellect? No.

Other children thought the stories were funny,
I suspect.
Black children felt bad that the others, it didn't affect.

Struggles seemed to have always been our plight,
But we trusted God and tried to do things right.

If You Only Knew Who I Am.

America was built by the American Indians and the Negro race,
But people forgot this and called themselves "putting us in our place."

GOD is in charge;
He sees no color.
Jesus said,
"We are to love one another."

I was raised to treat people right.
It made no difference if they were Black or White.
Dr. Martin Luther King
Did a good thing.
Some people will continue to hate,
Regardless of the fate.

Poetic Voices

God is a Spirit;
He has no color.
His will is that we would
Love one another.

"All Lives Matter" **BECAUSE**
"Jesus came to give us life!"

If You Only Knew Who I Am.

Sometimes, doors are often closed in our face
Because we are of a dark-skinned race.
Every minority whose life has been snuffed out…
Payday is coming to the offender — and that's no doubt.

God's Holy Word says,
"Thou shalt not kill."
Many won't listen,
And a very few will.

"I thank God that I can breathe!"

If You Only Knew Who I Am.

> *"I will praise Thee; for I am fearfully and wonderfully made: marvelous are thy works; and that my soul knoweth right well."*
> **~ Psalm 139:14 ~**

Poetic Voices

Black Woman Systematically
Tosha Dearbone

Tosha Dearbone was born in Urania, Louisiana, and raised in Houston, Texas. She is a mother of four, grandmother of one, Community Advocate, Mental Health Aid, Founder of Positive Express, Certified Medical Assistant, Certified Nursing Assistant, Certified Community Health Worker, Mentor, and an Author. Tosha specializes in medical care, educating young ladies and women about HIV and AIDS, domestic/sexual violence, self-esteem, and is a voice for breaking generational curses. Tosha found her passion for young ladies through her own testimony of traumatic youth experiences and building a relationship with God. Tosha can be reached on social media at Tosha R Dearbone and via email trdearbo@yahoo.com.

Poetic Voices

When asked, "Why is this not talked about?
Why is this not spoken?"
I cringed in my Black skin.
"It's meaningless to speak up when no one listens," she says.
There are times when I walk into the building,
Not knowing if stares are directed at the skin I am in or even the color of my hair.
The officer makes a remark,
"The color of your hair is a trigger to our White kids."
So, why talk about it?
No one listens.
All they see is the color of my skin and the color of my hair, yet no one sees the love so freely given.
I am a Black woman living in a systematic world,
Disregarded because of the color of my skin.
I get it.
It is superiority or inferiority that is defined by the color of my skin.
So, why talk about it?
Change will only come when we all can be recognized by one thing —
And that is **LOVE**…
Equally shown superior to our Black and White sisters and brothers.

I am a Black woman genuinely and systematically.

Poetic Voices

My Racially Mixed-Up Journey
Carl Reid

At the age of six,
I thought the races could mix.
A blonde-haired, blue-eyed girl; yes, I fell
For a schoolgirl named Adele.

My mother bought a ring I trusted
Would help me along the way with my crush.
Her parents took some time…
Then looked at me like I was slime.

Now grown and living in Maryland,
Eating a good meal —
But with the "N-word"
I still have to deal!
I'm now much bigger,
Yet on my job, two coworkers still called me a "Nigger"!

Still, I stand strong and proud,
Hoping this racism won't be my shroud!

Poetic Voices

Melting Pot
Angela R. Edwards

How very fortunate it was for me
To be raised in a small town and not the big city.
Surrounded by people of all different kinds
Served to show many shared the same mind.
If you were the one harboring hatred,
you were among the very few.
If you were the one harboring hatred,
what were you to do?
Humanity—with all its glorious colors—
stirs the melting pot daily.
I implore you to now seek a way
to stir the melting pot fairly.

Poetic Voices

A Prayer for a Brighter Day
Terrace White

Terrace V. White is a Richmond, Virginia-based first-time author of the non-fictional book *Parenting Memoir: From the Heart of a Single Father*. He retired from the United States Air Force in 2000, received the Gene Ackers Father of the Year Award in 2008 for Henrico County, Virginia, and has worked in the Logistics career field for the Federal Government for almost 20 years. He is a charismatic and dedicated single father who leads a daughter, stepdaughter, and son to realizing their life dreams. Terrace loves to inspire others, especially single parents, to believe in themselves, their parenting abilities and finding that right work/family balance.
Email: terracewhite7@gmail.com
Instagram: @ TerraceWhite7

Poetic Voices

Lord, reveal yourself to us that we see ourselves in You.
Give us a clear mind and clean heart through and through.
Hear our cry to break down these walls;
"Save our neighborhoods" is our loudest call.

The road to equality is long and hard.
The lives of black men they foolishly disregard.
Stunned by their guns and silenced when we talk,
Nothing will hold us back because we ask, seek, and knock.

Treat all men equal — the so-called law requires.
Guide us, Oh Lord; Your people's hands are tired.
Then, I remembered Your promises and I'm reminded of Your glory.
No longer do I see the injustice, but a different end to our story

Help us to stay focused on love and all Your creation.
Ensure we don't get detracted from the birth of a new nation.
Thriving, fruitful, and sense of community we keep;
A perfect example of what once was Black Wall Street.

Let Your people rise and claim their own.
Protect us, use us, and let Your will be done.
Praise be to God for restored hope and faith,
As we proudly sing and march to see a brighter day!

Poetic Voices

The Tenacity To...
Angela R. Edwards

I casually stroll down the sidewalk,
And you have the tenacity to cross the street.

You see me approaching and divert your eyes,
While having the tenacity to grip your purse tighter.

When my children are misbehaving,
You have the tenacity to think they are not being raised correctly.

On the job, when I am promoted,
You have the tenacity to believe it is because of Affirmative Action and not my merit.

My dark skin, wavy hair, and thick curves are my blessing,
Yet you have the tenacity to despise me while desiring elements of my blackness.

My people live with the threat and fear of being harmed because of the skin we are in,
Yet you still have the tenacity to make false claims that jeopardize our very lives.

CONVERSELY...

Poetic Voices

When I am called a n****r or other derogatory names,
I have the tenacity to feel sorry for those who display a lack of knowledge concerning the uses and definitions of those words.

When I see you, I greet you with a genuine smile — even if it is not returned —
For in my rearing up, I have the tenacity to believe you are no better than I.

When I hold the door for you and do not receive so much as a simple "Thank you,"
I have the tenacity to consider that some people live with a heightened sense of entitlement…as if I were *OBLIGATED* to oblige.

Even amid the racial turmoil that is encamped around my family and me daily,
I **STILL** choose to acknowledge the good in others and pray the day will come when we *ALL* have the tenacity to acknowledge we are *ALL* children of the Most High God, created in His image and likeness.

Poetic Voices

HANDS UP!
Marlowe R. Scott

People of all races are demanding recognition and justice,
Especially for Black lives murdered by those sworn to protect us.

Chants are heard, saying, "Black Power" and "Black Lives Matter,"
As people raise their arms during marches, rallies, and protests with lots of vocal chatter.

The cause of the marches and resulting signs and speeches
Began when authorities murdered a Black man by taking his breath away.
His pleas of "HELP" went unheeded, as witnesses were there that awful day!

Now, there are demands for justice and an end to blatant racism—
Demands heard not only from the USA, but also countries far away.

How different things were when I was a child;
I was taught to raise my hand to ask permission or answer a question.
Now, as an adult worshipping, singing, and praising,
My hands reach toward Heaven and join others whose hands are also raising.

Poetic Voices

We are all God's family, wrapped and protected with His love and blessings.
God defends us from the pains and racial hatred,
This world's disappointments and rejections.

We must press forward with prayers raised daily for justice and changes in humanity,
That some day soon, there will be an end to all this current brutality and insanity!!!

Poetic Voices

#45
John Hansboro

No, I'm not "scurred," but I think it's absurd
That our president's words kicked us to the curb.
When will they learn
They just want us to burn?

You turn on your TV, and Black men are beaten.
Your heart just starts grieving…this goes on all season.
So, we are all affected.
Don't you get the message?

They just dropped a bomb…
Now, everyone's gone.
It could have been prevented.
I think he's just venting.

Poetic Voices

Our prior presidents were cool under fire,
And they said, "He's a liar!"
But what you conspired — the home of The Wire —
Will leave you so tired.

Is that where they riot?
Are you for it or biased?
Let's not be divided.

The lines on the ground showed
How they killed Brown people of color,
even someone's mother.
When she was discovered, they said she had been smothered
By excessive force…yet, there's no remorse.

Can you keep your poise
Among all the noise?
Can you protect your family?
I know they can't stand me
Because I'm still standing — not going anywhere.
There's no harm or fear,
But our time is here…
So, let me be clear:
I don't want to hear your words.
They just sear.

The surface of purpose,
The kids out here lurking;
They took an innocent person's life
Coming home from working
A long day on the job.
They didn't expect to be robbed!

Poetic Voices

The family is scared,
Writing letters to mayors.
A young lion is scared;
Doesn't know he's a king.
Won't get into the ring
To settle a thing.

Poetic Voices

The DIAMOND of DIAMONDS
Terrance Bernard

The Story

There are many diamonds thrown away every day—all races, all nationalities— due to simple mistakes that anyone can make. Some people know how to hide well while breaking the law daily. Some of them are people with power and money. Others are ones who may convict one another. I believe that sometimes, the years for a crime are too much…which can corrupt a person even more. Only a few people may find themselves after so many years. Their lives become a cycle because after so long, some inmates never adapt to society again.

This is only my opinion, but I'm glad I found myself. I am the **DIAMOND** of *DIAMONDS*.

I dedicate my writing to all inmates around the world. Think about my words and find yourself.

Poetic Voices

I found a DIAMOND in the trash can;
The judge had thrown it away.
She thought the DIAMOND was worthless,
And so did the court's D.A.

The D.A. told her it had no value,
So she pondered over it for a moment.
The lawyer said to salvage it,
But the judge chose to disown it.

The sad thing about this case
Is that the DIAMOND had sat for years.
If the DIAMOND knew how to cry,
It may have shed many tears.

Now, as I look back at my life
And think about this judge:
Why did she throw me away?
Where were her heart and love?

I finally found myself
But feel I've lost my shine.
One day, I'll be free again;
For now, I'll leave you with this line:

"I FOUND MYSELF! Remember me…
I am the DIAMOND of DIAMONDS!"

The moral of the story here is that DIAMONDS find themselves when they SHINE!

Poetic Voices

A Mother's Prayer
Keywana Wright

A Mother Prays for her children always; she covers them in her heart and guards them from all harm.

A Mother Prays for her children; she sees danger from afar off and called them name by name.

A Mother's Prayer can open doors for her children when it comes to employment, education, financial gain, and all the benefits of life.

A Mother's Prayer can counsel a child who has strayed away and allowed alcohol and substances to take control over their mind; she will pray over their mind and that the habit cease.

A Mother's Prayer can bring hope to a child who feels hopeless.

A Mother's Prayer can bring healing to a child who has an illness or disease in his or her body.

A Mother's Prayer can open prison doors and set her child free.

A Mother's Prayer can bring peace to a child who is peaceless.

A Mother's Prayer can bring salvation to a child who needs to be saved.

Poetic Voices

A Mother's Prayer can bring a positive outcome in a neglectful situation.

A Mother's Prayer can bring the impossible in her child's life to the possible, just by asking God to do it.

A Mother's Prayer can move mountains.

Poetic Voices

Battle Tone
Poetless Shakespeare

What is freedom?
Is it really worth anything,
When so many have died
Not knowing what it means
To be free in the first place?

What is justice?
Is it another word that's
Supposed to describe our
Rights to be equal
In a society that won't even respect us…
Let alone recognize us?

We were birthed into a nation
That told us our freedom
Was just a façade of happiness.

Without any sense,
We gladly feasted upon
The lies they fed us
And became content in the
Hell they tossed us in.

Like corpses, we linger in the hollow glow
Of an undefeated battle
That leaves us helpless.

Poetic Voices

Martin had a dream to end war
And bring upon peace,
While Malcolm had a plan to see it out…
BY ANY MEANS NECESSARY.

The Black Panthers joined forces,
With fists held high
As a sign of strength.

What has happened to our nation?
Have we forgotten we were the cause
For the reproduction of greatness?

Our ancestors were killed,
Just for us to SAY the word "Freedom."

Poetic Voices

Dying Words
Marlowe R. Scott

I can't breathe! I can't breathe!
Words of a dying Black man.

I can't breathe! I can't breathe!
Someone, please help me!
I know you can!

I can't breathe! I can't breathe!
I see my Mother's hand.

I can't breathe! I can't breathe!
Now, I'm entering
God's Heavenly Land!

Poetic Voices

Fast-Forward to 2021
Marilyn E. Porter

In 2021, I will be sure to let the sun shine on my face plenty 'cause I've been shut up behind closed doors and windows in 2020.

In 2021, I will be certain to see my Mother's face more often and hear the vibration of my children's voices 'cause in 2020, I was separated from the two against my own deciding.

In 2021, I am going to remember someone needlessly lost their stay here on the planet because they were in the wrong time, wrong space…or just the wrong race.

Breanna and George lost their lives to remind us…

Fast forward to 2021, 2022, 2023…

Dear God, never let me get so caught up in what's going on out there that I fast forward past ME. It is the inner ME that keeps my heart centered and my mind clear so that I can remember:

2020 is but a number. It's just another year.

So, let's be done with it now.

Get up, Dear One. You can't stay down.

I repeat: *Fast forward to 2021.*

Poetic Voices

Who Would Have Dreamed It?
Marlowe R. Scott

Who was it that dreamed a precious baby girl born October 20, 1964, would one day rise to the second-highest office in the USA—a baby of mixed races, who would grow to be an achiever in many ways? She is a woman with outstanding accomplishments in legal and governmental positions.

Who Would Have Dreamed It?

Primarily raised by her mother, Gopalan, from the country of India, who taught Kamala valuable lessons of self-worth, speaking up, and standing up for not only herself, but also others. Kamala was an outgoing, respected young girl. Early on, it was recognized that she could be depended on. Her time to shine would now come to the forefront.

Who Would Have Dreamed It?

Many factors are affecting not only Black USA citizens, but also various races and sexes of all humankind. The primary reasons for injustice stemmed from leaders of Kamala's beloved USA — those who are self-centered, ill-prepared, and misusing their power and position to make others suffer.

Who Would Have Dreamed It?

Poetic Voices

The time came for the USA to choose someone to stand with the Democratic Party's Presidential Nominee, Joe Biden—a running mate as Vice President of the USA. Many women were qualified and interviewed, but Kamala came to the front as Joe Biden's choice, thus becoming the **FIRST** woman of color as well as the **FIRST** woman chosen for that honor!

Who Would Have Dreamed It?

Much like the story in the biblical Book of Esther, Kamala was in place to help save not only her race but a nation from death and destruction.

With Kamala by his side, Democratic Party Presidential Nominee, Joe Biden, and the USA are being refreshed and ready to move forward. It's time to reach the goal of getting the USA back to the nation for its people, fairly governed by the people—just as the Constitution clearly states.

Kamala, continue to be a strong, honest, supportive force to **SPEAK UP, SPEAK OUT,** and **BE HEARD** in the USA and throughout the world!

Who Would Have Dreamed It?

Poetic Voices

Conclusion

There comes a time when one must take a stand against racial injustice and inequality. That time is now. Here's the thing, though: The fight has always existed for the Black community. Dating to the early times of slavery, when Black people were snatched from their country, enslaved, and forced to serve their "master," they have always found a way to survive…or die trying. Their struggle will never be forgotten.

Sadly, the conversation concerning unfairness in the USA and around the globe is a topic that will likely never end — at least not in this lifetime. There will always be someone who gives a thumbs-down to equality. It is those people who need a change of heart, not those who scream, **"YOU WILL HEAR ME!"**

From our youth to our older generation, this book has shown that racism, fascism, totalitarianism, and a host of other "isms" are accepted as ridiculous norms. However, the contributors to *Poetic Voices* have realized their voices will not be silenced; they refuse to embrace others' norms as their way of life. It is in that space where change begins for not only them, but for you (the reader) as well.

As mentioned in the Introduction, you are encouraged to share the messages contained herein. Let others know they are not alone. The Holy Bible states there is **NOTHING** new under the sun (Ecclesiastes 1:9), which means that even before "now," the struggle was a part of life for our ancestors, and their ancestors, and…you get the point, right? Tell our young people that dying at the hands of those charged to protect isn't *NORMAL*. Black parents should not have to live in fear for their children as they go about being "kids." Spouses and significant others shouldn't have to fear being snatched out of cars and shot dead on the spot "just because." Those things are unacceptable and will no longer be tolerated.

WE. WILL. NOT. BE. SILENT.

Yes, all lives matter, but that's not the point here. "**BLACK LIVES MATTER**" is the cry, all because we are treated unfairly and continue to be looked down on as if our existence were some type of fluke…a mistake…a flaw. Guess what?

GOD MAKES NO MISTAKES!

It is our sincerest hope and earnest prayer that something you read here encouraged you to fight another day.

USE YOUR VOICE to **FIGHT** for your rights!

USE YOUR VOICE to **FIGHT** for equality!

USE YOUR VOICE to **FIGHT** for justice!

USE YOUR VOICE to **FIGHT** for your very *LIFE*!

Then, when you're tired and feel as if you don't have the strength to take one more step or utter one more word, stop and think of **ALL** those who used their **VOICE** and sacrificed their lives so that you *COULD*.

Poetic Voices

Meet the Collaborators

Angela R. Edwards

Angela R. Edwards is the CEO and Chief Editorial Director of Pearly Gates Publishing, LLC (PGP) and Redemption's Story Publishing, LLC (RSP) — Award-Winning International Christian Book Publishing Houses located in Houston, Texas. In May 2018, PGP was honored as the 2018 Winner of Distinction for Publishing in South Houston, Texas, by the Better Business Bureau (BBB). Ever since 2018, she has been awarded BBB Gold Star Certificates for both entities for her exemplary service to the community.

Poetic Voices

Angela's mantra is ***"My Words Have POWER!"*** Since its inception in January 2015, PGP has been blessed with an ever-growing and diverse group of almost 100 authors who have penned topics related to faith, love, abuse, bullying, Bible study tools, marriage, and so much more. Their youngest author is only three years old; their eldest is 76 years old at the time of this publication. To their credit and God's glory, PGP and RSP collectively have over 150 best-selling titles to date.

An affordable publishing option (in comparison to some of the large, traditional publishing houses), PGP and RSP work one-on-one with authors to ensure that financial hardship is not a discouraging part of the publishing process. For those desiring to share their God-inspired messages for the masses, to include both new and 'seasoned' authors, both publishing houses provide unique services and support that many have said "left them feeling as if they are the only author" placed under each company's care.

The Holy Bible states that *"God loves a cheerful giver"* (2 Corinthians 9:7). To that end, PGP and RSP are frequently found hosting fantastic giveaways. Throughout the past few years, new author contests have awarded authors over $14,000.00 in products and services total.

Poetic Voices

In addition to the aforementioned, Angela is a domestic abuse survivor. Since first telling her abuse-survivor story publicly, she has become a 'Trumpet for Change.' She established the **"Battle-Scar Free Movement"** — an online community of individuals who freely express and share their own overcoming-testimonies while, at the same time, begin the vital healing process of the heart, mind, and soul. As part of her God-given mission, she provides abuse victims and survivors a **FREE** opportunity to anonymously share their testimonies in a book series entitled *God Says I am Battle-Scar Free*. Although the series will be completed in the Spring of 2021, Angela's mission to help individuals heal with the power of their words will continue. Assisting others with the healing process is paramount to her, which propelled her into becoming a volunteer Mentor for the Star of Hope Mission in Houston, Texas.

Angela holds an A.A. Degree in Business Administration from the University of Phoenix and is pursuing her B.S. Degree in Psychology with a concentration in Christian Counseling from LeTourneau University. She is a woman of God, wife, mother, grandmother of 12, daughter, sister, and trusted friend. Originally a New Jersey native, she has since made Texas her home and embraced the southern culture in

Poetic Voices

all its fullness. She loves life and affirms daily:

"NOT TODAY, SATAN… AND TOMORROW ISN'T LOOKING TOO GOOD FOR YOU, EITHER!"

Poetic Voices

Marlowe R. Scott

Marlowe R. Scott was born 1944 to the late Carl and Helena Harris. She is the youngest of three and the sole surviving sibling, a mother of three, a grandmother of five, and a great-grandmother of twelve. As a child, Marlowe always loved animals and nature in general. Before attending school, she learned how to read and memorized many of the rhyming stories in Mother Goose books.

With her parents and brothers, Marlowe attended John Wesley Methodist Church in Bridgeton, New Jersey, where she learned hymns, went to Sunday School and Methodist Youth Fellowship, and sang in the Junior Choir. A special memory she has is of when, during the Civil Rights Movement of the 1960s, she participated in a nonviolent march from the church to the Bridgeton County Courthouse steps.

Marlowe was taught the value of confidence early in her youth. The familiar words still ring true and are often spoken today by others:

*"You are no better than anyone else,
and nobody is better than you."*

Teachers enjoyed having her in classes, as she was intelligent, participated, and articulated very well. In 1962, when she was a Senior in Bridgeton High School, she was chosen to be the Lead Speaker in the graduation voice choir, which quoted a portion of Ecclesiastes 3.

Later, as a member of Friendship A.M.E. Church in Browns Mills, New Jersey, Marlowe taught Sunday School, sang in various choirs, ushered, and worked with the Missionaries. She was also the Pastor's Steward to the first woman pastor of the church. Because of her experiences, she was elected Lay President of the Atlantic City District of New Jersey of the 1st Episcopal District of the A.M.E. Church. The Atlantic City District had 31 churches she visited, and she was

Poetic Voices

charged with coordinating events, as well as other religious activities.

Marlowe retired from the workforce after 33 years of government civil service. She has found her voice now through writing inspirational books and poetry. She has penned the following Best-Selling books, which are available through Pearly Gates Publishing's website and Amazon:

- ❖ Spiritual Growth: From Milk to Strong Meat
- ❖ Keeping It Real: The Straight and Narrow
- ❖ Believing Without Seeing: The Power of Faith
- ❖ Worth the Journey: The Train Ride to Glory *(A trilogy of the three listed above)*
- ❖ Never Alone: Intimate Times with Jesus
- ❖ Plentiful Harvest: Fertile Ground
- ❖ I AM Cares: His Eyes Are on the Sparrow
- ❖ Abiding is Not Hiding: Safe in His Arms
- ❖ Pentecost: Where the Spirit of God Is
- ❖ Talli's Ancestry Surprise: Beginning the Ancestral Search *(A children's/family book)*

Poetic Voices

A personal theme Marlowe has adopted for her life is the Serenity Prayer:

"God, grant me the **SERENITY** to
accept the things I cannot change,
the **COURAGE** to change
the things I can,
and the **WISDOM**
to know the difference."

Poetic Voices

Pen A Poem

How do you *honestly* feel about these tumultuous times in our world's history? You are encouraged to release your deepest thoughts right here…right now. Take a moment to free-write your way to freedom from heartache and pain. It doesn't have to rhyme. It doesn't even have to make sense. Just let "it" go! You will begin to see the power of your own words flow from your mind down to your fingertips. Then, when you are ready, share what you've written with others.

*Together, let's be the **POETIC VOICES** of change the world needs today!*

Poetic Voices

Poetic Voices

Poetic Voices

Poetic Voices

Poetic Voices

Poetic Voices

Poetic Voices

Poetic Voices

www.ingramcontent.com/pod-product-compliance
Lightning Source LLC
Chambersburg PA
CBHW052119110526
44592CB00013B/1675